# Parents and Teachers

# Equipping the Younger Saints

## David Walters

Published by
**GOOD NEWS FELLOWSHIP MINISTRIES**
**220 Sleepy Creek Rd.**
**Macon, GA 31210**

**Phone (478) 757-8071**
**Fax (478) 757-0136**

**E-mail: goodnews@reynoldscable.net**
**www.goodnews.netministries.org**

Sixth Printing, July 2004

Published by
**GOOD NEWS FELLOWSHIP MINISTRIES**
**220 Sleepy Creek Rd.**
**Macon, GA. 31210**
Telephone: (478) 757-8071
Fax: (478) 757-0136
E-mail: goodnews@reynoldscable.net
http://www.goodnews.netministries.org

Unless otherwise noted, all Scripture quotations
are from the New King James Version of the Bible.
Copyright © 1979,1980,1982
by Thomas Nelson Inc., publishers.
Used by permission.

Scripture quotations marked KJV are from
the King James Version of the Bible.

**OTHER TITLES**
**By David Walters:**

Kids in Combat
Children Aflame
Revival Anointing & You
Worship fur Dummies
Radical Living in a Godless Society
Being a Christian
Children's Prayer Manual
Fact or Fantasy
Fruit of the Spirit
The Armor of God

# CONTENTS

# INTRODUCTION

Did you ever wonder if your church-wise children can be turned around and set on fire for God? Are you ready for your teenagers to stop succumbing to peer pressure and start being the peers? Do you want to see your kids 100 percent committed to Christ, filled with the Spirit and moving in the gifts?

David and Kathie Walters have spent the past twenty years traveling and speaking about the anointing of God to children, teenagers, Sunday school teachers and youth pastors. Originally from England, they presently reside in Macon, Georgia, with their two daughters, Faith and Lisa. When they minister, they expect children as young as six (sometimes younger) to receive the Holy Spirit and exercise the gifts of the Spirit. They have seen youngsters prophesy, have visions and dreams, use the word of knowledge, pray for the sick and administer healing.

Young people do not receive a baby or junior Holy Spirit. They are baptized in the Holy Spirit to do much more than mutter a few syllables of a prayer language. When we adults exclude the children from spiritual activity, we can exclude a move of the Spirit. But by acknowledging that God will use the little ones, we take a blow to our pride, and there is more room for God.

What David Walters is sharing is not just a theory about children's ministry or a revelation on the meaning of certain scriptures. It is based on what he has seen God do with children and what he continues to see Him do everywhere he travels.

The purpose of this book is to impart a vision and anointing to parents and youth leaders so that they may equip their children and youth to become mighty in the Spirit for God. Chapter 1 describes what Christian parents need to do to raise godly children (we can't raise anointed kids unless we are anointed ourselves!). The goal is true salvation. After that children can be baptized in the Holy Spirit, and parents and church leaders can guide them into spiritual gifts. Walters explains in detail how the Bible says the gifts of the Spirit operate and how he has seen them operate in children through his own ministry.

Some material in this book may seem revolutionary, but that is because it is so different from the way children's and youth ministries are being conducted right now. So if you want to see more vision, power and commitment in your youth, be prepared to lay aside old traditions and expect God to work radically through you!

Walter L. Walker
Editorial Director
Creation House

# ONE

# RAISING GODLY CHILDREN

C hristian parents hope and pray their children will turn out to be good kids and not go astray. Their secret prayer is that the Lord will enable them to raise their children to stay away from trouble, such as bad company, drugs, illicit sex, heavy rock music and rebellion. They hope their children will eventually find successful careers, settle down and marry good partners.

I believe all of us as Christian parents want that for our children, and we hope the church can assist us in bringing this about. Unfortunately, the days we live in are far more difficult and sinful than they were a few years ago. The moral standard of our country has decreased tremendously in the last twenty-five years.

Trying to encourage or teach our kids to be merely good and moral is not enough. With the breakdown in the home, with so many parents getting divorces, with apathetic believers, Christian leaders falling into sin and splits in the churches, our children have very few, if any, godly role models to follow. Coupled with that, the media and the secular community portray Christianity as old-fashioned, wimpy, bigoted and restricting. It is no wonder our youngsters are having a hard time.

In these days we have to go beyond raising good kids to raising anointed ones. Just being good is sometimes boring and no fun. I tell children — and they agree with me — that it is much more fun being naughty than good. God does not expect our youngsters to be good for the sake of being good. He expects them to be good to qualify them to become mighty.

Unless our children receive a real vision of God, who He is, what He has done for them and what He has destined them to become, we will lose them. It has been stated that 80 percent of all church-raised kids in the Western world leave the church by the time they become adults. This is the generation that we are fighting to save.

How can we as parents raise our youngsters to be mighty for God? Are single parents able to accomplish this as well as couples?

The Bible makes an interesting statement about John the Baptist: "He will also be filled with the Holy Spirit, even from his mother's womb" (Luke 1:15b). A Spirit-filled baby! How interesting. But that was John the Baptist, you might say. Our children are not John the Baptists. But Jesus said, "Among those born of women there is not a greater prophet than John the Baptist; but he who is least in the kingdom of God is greater than he" (Luke 7:28).

Well! Are our children in the kingdom of God? We know that youngsters at a given point in time must repent of their sins and accept Christ as their Savior. We also know that babies cannot understand the gospel with their minds and repent of their sins until they reach an age of accountability. Yet they do have spirits, and although we cannot teach very much about God to their minds initially, we can feed (or destroy) their spirits.

For example, if infants are raised in a hostile, negative environment where there is violence, strife, anger and discord, their spirits will be damaged and devastated. They may not understand the words being screamed and shouted, but their spirits will pick up the negative atmosphere that has been created. If this continues as they grow older, it will be very difficult for them to accept the Lord. They will need much counseling and probably deliverance before they make any headway with God.

On the other hand, if an infant has been exposed to the peace, harmony, love and presence of the Holy Spirit, that child will probably accept Jesus easily when he or she becomes accountable. Why? Because his or her spirit has been fed and nurtured. The verse that says "train up a child in the way he should go" depicts stimulating a child's appetite for God, as a mother stimulates the palate of a newborn child for milk, that it will take nourishment (see Prov. 22:6).

If parents learn how to minister the presence of the Lord to their infants in a godly atmosphere at home, those children will develop a hunger and desire for the presence of God when they are brought to church. Here's what you can do.

1. Spend time with your infants in the things of God.

2. Sing worship songs to them or play worship tapes.

3. Read the Word of God to them, regardless of whether they understand.

4. Pray over them and break any curses they may have inherited from their family ancestry. Many families have some negative history in their background that can affect their little ones. "For I, the Lord your God, am a jealous God, visiting the iniquity [curses] of the fathers upon the children to the third and fourth generations of those who hate Me" (Deut. 5:9).

I have been criticized by some people who claim that exposing small children to my kind of ministry is too scary for them, especially because of the graphic descriptions I use when explaining the crucifixion, the cost of following Christ and what happens to unbelievers. I have been told they are not ready to be serious followers of the Lord. If this is true, why does Satan attack our children in the womb with attempted abortion? Also, remember Satan's attempt to destroy Moses and Jesus as infants through Pharaoh and King Herod (see Ex. 1:15-22, 2:1-3; Matt. 2:16). Then, when children are older, he attacks them with occultic violent cartoons and negative role models such as Bart Simpson, Teenage Mutant Ninja Turtles and Care Bears.

Our children need to be equipped with God's armor from the crib. Satan is not waiting for our cute little kids to become older before he goes after them. They have been born into the war zone and need to be dressed for battle. Regardless of what many mothers may think, childhood is not all pink roses and butterflies.

In our ministry to children and youth we have often seen tiny ones from the nursery come into our meetings and be overcome by the presence of God. Often they are transfixed for long periods of time as the Holy Spirit ministers to their spirits. They do not understand with their minds all that is happening, but their spirits recognize the presence of God and desire Him. A church nursery can become a wonderfully supernatural infant ministry if the nursery workers and parents know how to minister the presence of the Holy Spirit among the little ones.

As parents we cannot raise anointed kids if we are not anointed ourselves. This means *more* than just feeling the presence of the Lord or relying on the Holy Spirit when we are in a church meeting. It means being anointed at home in the domestic scene, being able to discipline our children and run the house in the Spirit. Having spiritual authority is higher than parental or ecclesiastical authority. That kind of authority may produce outward obedience, but true spiritual authority deals with the child's inner man and breaks the spirit of rebellion that is often controlling him.

In other words, if we minister to our children in the flesh, we will have negative results, but if we remember to stay in the Spirit (anointing), then raising our children will become much more profitable (see Is. 10:27; Rom. 8:1-2; Eph. 6:4). You may say, It's very hard for me to stay or even get in the Spirit. Our home is so often in a turmoil, and the kids are always bickering with each other. Plus I can never get them to obey me. My husband does not help (or I don't have a husband, I'm a single parent). Walking in the Spirit is a revelation rather than a struggle. Many of us are trying to qualify to walk in the Spirit by achieving victory over the flesh. Let me show you some steps to take to walk in the Spirit.

1. Make a decision to walk in the Spirit by faith.

2. Refuse to lose your peace. You will soon realize that people do not upset you, but you upset yourself, when you give up your peace.

3. Pray every morning for the Lord's peace to fill your home, your life and the lives of your children.

4. Check very carefully what enters your home through magazines, TV and music.

5. Do not allow the enemy to break through and cause sin, confusion and discord to run rampant in your house.

6. Learn to hate sin with a passion and beware of compromise.

7. Also learn to hate sickness as much as sin so it will not plague your door. (Many Christian people welcome sickness as an old friend and at the first symptom accept it as the inevitable.)

Very soon you will have created, by the Holy Spirit, an atmosphere of peace, harmony and health in your home that even visitors will notice when they enter the house. Remember, the enemy will continue to attack you to wear you down. Don't be a crybaby or a wimp, pleading with the devil to leave you alone. Stand up to him and say, "Come on, Satan. I love a good fight, for I'm called to be a mighty warrior for God, and His Word says you are a defeated foe" (see Luke 10:18-19).

Catherine Booth, the wife of the Salvation Army founder William Booth, was raised by godly parents. She had read the Bible through many times before she reached the age of twelve. She followed through with those principles after she was married and, with her husband, raised six children. As a result, all of their children ended up in full-time service for the Lord.

Charles Spurgeon, the famous preacher of the last century, wrote a book called *Come, Ye Children.*[1] Many times in the book he states that children should be taught the whole counsel of God as soon as they are old enough for Sunday school. He says that the younger a child is converted to Christ the better, and the younger they are taught to serve Him the better. He did not believe in waiting until they were older before challenging them to accept Christ. Although he was criticized for his stance by many, he still maintained his convictions.

It is worth noting that when Spurgeon was eleven years of age he was reading books on theology. By the time he was fifteen he was preaching in churches, and by the time he was seventeen he was pastoring a church. When he had reached the grand old age of nineteen, he was pastoring the largest church in England. In fact, the Metropolitan Tabernacle where he pastored had to be expanded to cope with the crowds that were attending. While the church was being renovated he moved into the famous Crystal Palace in London, where he drew crowds of more than ten thousand. Many of the London preachers were very put out that a nineteen-year-old should have so much fame.

Today we see many youngsters becoming famous and making a name for themselves in the rock music world (most of them doing Satan's work). Yet we see so few youngsters becoming firebrands and leaders for God among their own peers. This has to change if we are going to save and equip this generation.

"Train up a child in the way he should go, and

when he is old he will not depart from it" (Prov. 22:6). This verse also means that a child follows the parents' dictates until he has qualified for independency, regardless of his age. I tell older kids and teens that in God's eyes having the right to be independent and leave home doesn't automatically happen when you reach the age of seventeen. In the same way, you are not qualified to drive a car, fly a plane, be a doctor or whatever just because you reach a certain age.

The Bible indicates that children qualify to become independent only after they have learned to *obey* their parents. By learning obedience they become responsible. If they refuse to do this, they could end up as prodigals (see Eph. 6:1-3; Col. 3:20; Heb. 5:8).

One of the major problems parents encounter with their children is rivalry between siblings. As I have stated elsewhere, children are usually self-centered or selfish. Part of training children is to break that natural condition. We know their carnal nature cannot be improved, so it is no good appealing to that. They, like us, have to learn to put off the old man and put on the "new man" and "walk in the Spirit" (see Eph 4:22-24; Gal. 5:16).

The first thing parents must do is set godly standards and rules so the children learn quickly what is permissible and what is not. It is no good expecting them to be able to make the right choices or do the right things just because the parents are Christians. They must have a correct formula to follow.

If they begin to behave or talk in a carnal way, it's good practice to ask the question, Is that the old or the new man speaking? This checking on

13

each other could be good for the whole household.

My feelings about teaching children, as you have probably realized by now, is that children need to *know* God. If their theology is faulty, then faulty behavior will follow. Obviously children must have the desire to live a victorious Christian life and not just say yes because that is what is expected of them. The following scripture and example will help you explain this concept to children: "For the law of the Spirit of life in Christ Jesus has made me free from the law of sin and death" (Rom. 8:2). The law of sin and death is like gravity. It pulls us down and keeps us earthbound. As long as we live on this earth we are subject to gravity. Gravity will always be with us. No matter how much kids would like to be able to float or fly in the air, gravity will not allow them to do that. The law of sin and death will always be with us. No matter how much we would like sin and temptation to be taken away so we could be good and perfect, it will not happen while we live in this world.

But God has made a way. When we become true Christians — including kids — we receive the law of the Spirit of life, which is like the law of aerodynamics, which keeps a plane flying. Although the law of gravity is still there, another law, the law of aerodynamics, is brought into being, which supersedes the gravity law. As long as that law is operating, the plane defies the law of gravity. In the same way, as long as *we allow* the law of the Spirit of life to operate in us, then we are free from the law of sin and death. Remember! What you believe rules you. You do not rule your believing. That's why it's more important to find out what our children and teens really believe than to merely have them obey.

There are a number of parents who believe that small children or even older ones should not be pressured into accepting Christ until they are ready. Some even allow their children to make their own decisions about coming to church or not, for fear of turning them off or making them hate God. They do not believe in disciplining their children spiritually, yet they do not give them a choice about attending school, brushing their teeth, eating their vegetables or keeping clean. Even if the child protests and claims that he hates school, brushing his teeth and so on, he is still made to do it. I have often preached in churches where parents have come to me after the meetings, saying how they wished their child had been present, but he or she did not want to come. When I have asked how old the child is, I have been given ages ranging from nine to seventeen.

Parents! It is not enough just to get our children to church on Sundays. They also need to be involved in praise and worship and ministry. Too many kids and teens just attend and never enter in. They look on with a bored and disinterested attitude. They can't wait for the service to finish so they can go outside and play or hang around with their friends.

Evelyn Hamon, wife of Bill Hamon, president and founder of the Christian International Network of Prophetic Ministries, tells how she as a mother made it very clear to her four children when they were young that there would be no discussion about *not* going to church. They would always be there when the doors were open. Not only that, but she expected them to enter in. If they refused to raise their hands and praise the Lord, she would pinch them under the elbows until they did. She said the congregation would see her children with their hands raised in the air and tears running down their faces and say, "Look at the anointing on those children."

"It wasn't the anointing," she said. "They were in pain."

If she did that kind of thing today she would probably be reported for child abuse, but the strange thing is that her children did not end up hating God or despising church. They are all in full-time ministry for the Lord.

When we bring our little ones to church, we as parents must train them to behave, especially if they have to be in a meeting with adults. Many parents let them run around all over the church and make a racket. Because of this, too many children are confused and think they are in a playground or nursery. Small children need to be taught right away what church is.

One of the best ways to explain what church is is to explain to them what it isn't. I ask, What is a church? Is it a playground? They shout, No! Is it Disney World? No! Is it a nursery? No! Is it a swing park? No! Is it a racetrack? No! Finally I say, It's a place where we meet and worship God and are taught how to be His champions.

Children *can* sit still for long periods of time. I tell them that when they are in my meetings they don't have to squiggle; they *can* sit still. They won't die if they sit still; they really won't. They *can* do it.

It usually works. The religious leaders once complained to Jesus about the children crying out in the temple (Matt. 21:15-16). Most people do not like to hear children cry out in church. We all like them to behave. The interesting thing is that these children were not crying out because they were fussing and wanted to go to the nursery to play. No, they were crying out, "Hosanna to the Son of David!" How old were these little ones? Ten, eleven or twelve? It seems to me that many of them must have been between the ages of eighteen months and three years, otherwise Jesus could not have quoted accurately, "Out of the mouth of babes and nursing infants You have perfected praise." In the light of that statement I think it is safe to assume that many of the children were very young.

Christian parents must be careful *not* to sacrifice their children to the "god of education." What do you mean? you might ask. If my children are being deprived of spiritual growth due to the amount of study they have to do to achieve top grades to qualify for college, then I am in danger of sacrificing them to a false god.

Unfortunately, many Christian kids are missing opportunities to attend special meetings designed to empower them because of their school commitments. Some parents say, "I cannot bring my child to the Sunday evening meeting because it will go on late and they have to be fresh for school on Monday." That is believing their education is more important than their spiritual development. Other parents go even further and do not bring their children to meetings because they have football practice, cheerleading or music lessons.

I did a special series of children's meetings on a Friday evening and at an all-day Saturday workshop recently in a church. Although we had a good crowd, a number of children did not attend any of the meetings. I later had the opportunity of ministering to them at the Sunday morning meetings. Out of curiosity I asked why a number of them did not come to the meetings. The excuses I was given were surprising. The kids gave reasons from having football practice and visiting Grandma to going to parties and shopping at the mall. I could not blame the children, but I could see that their parents had a sad lack of revelation about spiritual empowerment for their children.

I meet many youth pastors and children's church teachers who become very frustrated with parents who do not seem to care about their children's spiritual welfare. On some occasions the children's pastor has been frustrated when I have been giving a training seminar for children's teachers and some of his children's teachers have not bothered to show up.

Some parents and teachers think they know what it's all about and are still living in the old traditions and concepts of teaching children spiritual things. Those old ideas are not working. That is why God is bringing about a fresh vision today, showing parents and children's teachers how to equip children to be mighty for God. Children have spirits which need to be fed.

People are tripartite beings — body, mind (soul) and spirit. Good parents look after children's physical needs by ensuring they have adequate food, sleep and exercise. They also make sure their minds are fed through education. Some Christian parents also feed their children's minds with some form of Christian education so that the youngsters will have a knowledge of the Bible and God.

We as parents and teachers have emphasized the first two parts but have often neglected the third.

Our children's spirits have been stunted. They can know about God with the mind, but they can only *know* God by the spirit. God is a Spirit; we have a spirit. Spirit to spirit (see Rom. 8:15-17). That is why so many of our kids know about God but don't know Him (see Dan. 11:32). When Jesus was a boy, what was He like? In Luke 2:40 we read, "And the Child grew and became strong in spirit, filled with wisdom; and the grace of God was upon Him" (also see 2 Cor.3:6; Gal.3:3).

While I was in Singapore recently I read a report about a number of teens who had committed suicide due to the pressure of trying to make top grades at school. Who said the only way to be successful in life is to get a college degree? Some youngsters may not be naturally smart academically, but they could be gifted with their hands in wood carving, pottery or art. Some may have a natural aptitude to become an entrepreneur in some business or other. Anyway, the most important road to success for our kids is to know God.

Please don't misunderstand me. I am not against education. A good education is very important, and if your child has a flair and a desire to reach the top academically, then praise the Lord. But it is not the most important thing in life. Jesus is (see Phil. 1:21).

If we desire our teenagers to be used by God today, think of how He used them in Bible times. Joseph had dreams from God of great things, which initially got him into trouble, but ultimately the dreams came to pass. Jeremiah, the young prophet, was called to prophesy to the nations. Samuel brought the word of judgment from the Lord to Eli the priest. David slew the giant Goliath when he was still just a lad. Mary, a young girl, received the greatest honor of any human when she was chosen to become the mother of Jesus. Timothy was called to the ministry in his youth.

Subsequently, many children and teens have been used by God down through history. A number have suffered torture and death rather than deny Christ. In Revelation 6:9-11 John sees the fifth seal opening and an altar of souls of those who have been slain for the Word of God and the testimony they held. They ask, "How long, O Lord, holy and true, until You judge and avenge our blood on those who dwell on the earth?" They were told they would rest a little longer until both the number of their fellow servants and their brethren, who would be killed as they were, was completed. Some of these martyrs include children and youth.

A couple of years ago I was visiting the man who led me to the Lord back in 1959. He lives in a small house in Amersham, Buckinghamshire, England. He pointed to a field outside his living room window. Way down at the end we could see a small monument. To my surprise he explained, "That commemorates the martyrdom of some little children who died for their faith a couple of hundred years ago."

# TWO

# TRUE
# SALVATION

The whole purpose of raising our children is that they may experience true salvation. We can put godly standards into our children, teach them Bible principles, teach them morals and take them to church with us, but salvation still has to come through the Lord touching their spirits inside. We need to pray that God will grant them the spirit of repentance (see 2 Tim. 2:25). Not just repenting when they goof off or mess up, but a true repentance as they see themselves as hell-deserving sinners who are unfit for God's kingdom. If our children do not receive a genuine conviction of sin, they will take salvation very lightly.

When I preach to kids, I tell them the cost of their salvation was very dear to God. He sent His only Son to die for them. He did not have ten sons. Just one. Would they be prepared to let their little brother or sister die to set free the world's worst sinner? I doubt it. Yet God's love was so great that He was willing to sacrifice His only begotten Son. It was the only thing He could do, because sin is so exceedingly sinful.

Jesus did not pay that terrible price to have a church full of bored, apathetic kids. His plan is not to raise up a bunch of ordinary kids like the ones in the world. He died and rose again to raise up extraordinary kids. Had there been an easier way to bring it about, then He would have done it. I tell children that because it cost God so much, it's going to cost them a lot. Salvation may be free, but it's not cheap.

When some of our kids hear the gospel message, their attitude is, Well, I guess I'll go along with it. I'm not all that keen about it, but I guess I had better try to obey. The apostle Paul had a revelation of the cross far superior to that. He said that he gloried in the cross. "But God forbid that I should glory, save in the cross of our Lord Jesus Christ, by whom the world is crucified unto me, and I unto the world" (Gal. 6:14, KJV).

Paul did not merely say he thought the cross of Christ was a good idea, or even a great idea, but he *gloried* in it. To him it was the most amazing, the most magnificent, the most stupendous act in history. It was the greatest drama, the greatest event, that the human mind could ever comprehend. Why did he react in that way? Because such an event brought God in and took man out. It tells us there is absolutely nothing we can do or need to do, except one thing. "Believe on the Lord Jesus Christ, and you will be saved" (Acts 16:31). The finished work of Christ — and only the finished work of Christ — on the cross was his hope. That's why he gloried in it. Our kids need to understand that.

Paul saw on the cross all the attributes of God's holy character being displayed. He saw God's perfect law, justice and righteousness being fulfilled. He saw God's perfect love, mercy and compassion being extended in fullness. Different attributes with apparent contradictions, working in perfect harmony through the death of Christ on the cross. As the psalmist says, "Mercy and truth have met together; righteousness and peace have kissed each other" (Ps. 85:10).

God's love, mercy and peace were poured out, yet His justice, wrath and righteousness were not violated. There on the cross the innocent One became guilty that the guilty ones might become innocent. God's love was demonstrated in that He gave His Son as a sacrifice for sin and sickness, and His anger and wrath was vindicated in that He punished His own Son.

Paul saw the lifeblood of the Son of God being shed to cleanse him from sin. He saw Christ as his substitute, his sin-bearer, his redeemer and healer, who set his spirit free. He saw in that supreme act the attractions of the world being crucified unto him, and himself being crucified from those worldly desires. He saw in Christ's death his own death. That is why he could say, "For to me, to live is Christ, and to die is gain" (Phil. 1:21).

That's the kind of revelation and understanding that is going to make our children stand against the onslaughts of Satan. When they receive that revelation, it will not be: For me, to live is video games, sports, rock music or entertainment, but Christ.

Parents, expose your children as much as possible to anointed, radical preaching, coupled with signs and wonders. Don't just rely on Bible stories and Sunday school curriculum. If ever I hear of a man or woman of God coming into town who has a powerful message on salvation and discipleship, I expose my girls to it. Although they have heard me preach many times and have taken active part in my meetings, I still want them to be exposed to others who have a heavy anointing. I know it can do nothing but good for them.

Water finds its own level. That is to say that children who are fellowshipping with carnal kids or only going to spiritually dead meetings that emphasize entertainment and activities over and above spiritual warfare are destined to settle down to the level of their surroundings. Make sure your children and teenagers have friends who are not going to pull them down spiritually. It's not only having non-Christian friends that causes this to happen. There are many carnal, church-wise kids around today, and if they are your child's best friends, then your child will suffer.

I try to explain to youngsters that if they want to become good at something, they need to be around people who are better at it than they are. For example, if your child wants to improve his tennis game, he needs to practice with someone who is better at the game than he is. His game can improve because he will be stretched by his opponent's talent. If he only plays with people who are not as good as he or are about the same, then there will be little or no challenge for him to improve his game.

What is true in the natural is also true in the spiritual. Encourage your kids to make friends with those who are on fire for God and who are more mature than they are. This will be a good source of positive peer pressure to challenge them to improve their walk with God.

When ministering to your children, beware that they don't just give you the answers you want to hear to keep you off their backs. Explain to them that true spiritual conversion is a miracle. It is more than making a decision, even though that comes into it.

In the old days people looking for salvation would pray and seek God until they had received His peace and assurance in their hearts. In other words, their assurance did not just rely on believing John 3:16. It was more than that. They sought God until they had experienced Romans 8:15: "For you did not receive the spirit of bondage again to fear, but you received the Spirit of adoption by whom we cry out, 'Abba, Father!' " Galatians 4:6 also says, "And because you are sons, God has sent forth the Spirit of His Son into your hearts, crying out, 'Abba, Father.' " Remember, all doctrine is to be experienced and not merely acquiesced.

Once your children have shown a genuine conversion, the next step is to disciple them. Involve them in a good church that will help you make your child mighty for God. Many children have all kinds of gifts and talents that they can use for the Lord. With help and training from a progressive church, there are many areas in dance, music, drama, mime and singing where they can be used to proclaim their faith.

Another area to consider is allowing them to go on short-term missions during term breaks. A number of youth and children's pastors have a heart for missions and often take youngsters with them overseas. Organizations such as King's Kids, Teen Mania and Youth With a Mission provide a great challenge and a significant missionary experience.

Church camps for children and youth should emphasize the Lord more than just having a fun time. Share with the leadership what you are expecting for your child and the kind of camp you would like them to attend. During the summer of 1992 I was speaking at a children's camp in the mountains of Colorado. God moved in a mighty way, and many miracles took place. The children were really excited.

Because we were high up in the mountains (about nine thousand feet), the transportation was limited, so the leaders asked if I would be willing to travel back to the church in one of the buses with the youngsters.

When we arrived, many of the children were anxious to introduce me to their parents. As I was also scheduled to speak at the main service on Sunday morning, they wanted their parents to bring them.

Some said, "This is our camp speaker, Mr. Walters. When he preached, God moved in an awesome way."

Others described exactly what happened: "We were all filled with the Spirit, and most of us could not stand and lots of miracles happened. Even a deaf girl heard!"

"That's wonderful," said some of the parents. "Did you enjoy the canoeing, basketball, tomahawk throwing and games?"

"Oh, yeah! They were all right," replied the kids, "but you should have seen the meetings. They were awesome. God is so real."

When children begin to see the power and reality of God, they become more excited about God than about the ordinary, fun things we so often prepare for them.

# THREE

# A GENUINE HOLY SPIRIT BAPTISM

B ut this is that which was spoken by the prophet Joel; And it shall come to pass in the last days, saith God, I will pour out of my Spirit upon all flesh: and your sons and your daughters shall prophesy, and your young men shall see visions, and your old men shall dream dreams: and on my servants and on my handmaidens I will pour out in those days of my Spirit; and they shall prophesy" (Acts 2:16-18, KJV).

Have you ever wondered what our children are being taught in Sunday school these days? Are those of us who are members of Pentecostal or charismatic churches, and who apparently believe in the supernatural gifts of the Holy Spirit, training our children and youth effectively?

The fear of manipulation is another reason some people and a number of churches do not emphasize the need for children to experience the baptism of the Spirit or spiritual gifts until they have reached adulthood. I believe protecting children in this way is a mistake. In one sense youngsters are manipulated by their adult peers all through their early years. As I have previously mentioned, they are made to go to school, brush their teeth, eat their vegetables, tidy their rooms and attend church. I'm sure that many other things are forced upon them, depending upon the rules of the particular families.

If children *could* make their own choices, most of them would not fulfill the obligations that are demanded of them from the adults. This is why the Scriptures say, "Train up a child in the way he should go, and when he is old he will not depart from it" (Prov. 22:6; see also 2 Tim. 3:15). We know that the baptism and the gifts are not an option but a necessity. Because of this, we need to encourage our children to seek for this blessing. We also need to provide any scriptural assistance we can to help them arrive at the destiny God has for their lives.

Most Spirit-filled churches teach youngsters about the baptism of the Spirit with the evidence of speaking in tongues, but often it stops there. Many of our children's attitudes are, "Oh, yes, we've done that!" In other words, it's been done and then forgotten, rather than experienced and then developed. There have been many testimonies in the past of people of all ages who received such a mighty baptism that they could not stop speaking in tongues for hours or even days. Many testified of the transforming power and experience of the Holy Spirit as He came upon them, their emotions being turned upside down with weeping, repenting, shaking, laughing, along with feelings of great love, joy and gratefulness to the Lord.

Have we as adults and parents encouraged our children to believe that the baptism of the Holy Spirit is something less than it really is? In our desire to give them the fullness of the Spirit, have we dragged a few syllables out of their mouths and claimed that as the evidence? The Lord showed me that it is like an engine being turned over a few times by the starter but never igniting. Many children, when encouraged to receive the Holy Spirit, manage to say a couple of words in an unknown strain for a few seconds and then stand around looking rather sheepish until they are dismissed.

My question is: Is this that which was spoken by the prophet Joel and confirmed by the apostle Peter? Is this the wonderful experience of God's power that we have been telling them about? Is this what all the fuss is about? If so, no wonder we have so many church-wise kids who are not turned on to the Lord. Children are not baptized in the Holy Spirit so they may play, be entertained or listen to a couple of moral object lessons. This experience should initiate them into a supernatural walk with God (see Acts 2:1-47).

Although moral object lessons are important for kids to learn, the anointing of God and the supernatural power of the Holy Spirit are always exciting. Children will respond when they have serious teaching and workshops on the gifts of the Holy Spirit. In fact, it is most important that the youngsters have a genuine Holy Spirit baptism. This subsequently opens them up to receive an impartation of the gifts and instills in them a hunger to be trained in how to continue to flow in the gifts and anointings of the Holy Spirit.

When children are baptized in the Holy Spirit, they are not given a pint-sized version of the Spirit. They are endued with the same power as the adults. Children will believe what adults tell them. If we teach them that the gifts of the Spirit are available to them and that God's desire is for them to move in the supernatural and become mighty, they will begin to respond accordingly (see Joel 2:28-29). If we imply that they are too young for these things, they will continue to goof off and not take the work of God seriously.

Many years ago in England I prayed for a young teenager named Nigel to receive the baptism. Nigel ended up bouncing all around the room on a chair shouting, "Bubbity, bubbity, bubbity." I thought, That sounds like a strange tongue to me. I wonder if it's real? I need not have been concerned. That experience brought Nigel into a place where the Lord was able to use him to bring revival among the youth in his church and also at the secular school he was attending.

During that same period a couple of teenage brothers came to our house to be prayed for. One played a guitar and sang. They both received a mighty baptism. The guitar player's name was Graham Kendrick, and he is now being used of the Lord internationally in Christian music.

Some time ago I was preaching at a large meeting of children in Florida. Many of them were baptized in the Spirit and could not stop speaking in tongues for hours. If I had not eventually closed the meeting, I believe they would have gone on all night.

I am personally challenged more and more to explain to children the need to really desire the fullness of the Holy Spirit in their lives — not to be content with just a little trickle, but to seek for a great well springing up within them. A twelve-year-old named Stephen was so desperate for the baptism that he tried everything. He read in the

Word about covering, so he put a handkerchief on his head and prayed, but nothing happened. Then he read about standing on the Word, so he stood on his Bible and prayed, and still nothing happened. But he kept on praying and seeking, and finally God baptized him in his bed. He couldn't stop speaking in tongues for many days.

As we have traveled through the body of Christ holding crusades, seminars and workshops for children and youth, we have witnessed God using children time and time again. We have seen them prophesying, giving messages in tongues, having visions and dreams, exercising the word of knowledge and praying for the sick (sometimes with amazing results, such as cripples getting out of wheelchairs). They have also become burdened for the lost and bold in their witnessing.

# FOUR

# BRINGING THE PRESENCE OF THE HOLY SPIRIT

Many pastors, elders, children's and youth ministers ask me *how* to bring youngsters and adults into the presence of God. Not all churches are at the same spiritual level, so it is easier for a person to minister the Holy Spirit in some churches than in others. I have found, however, that the Holy Spirit will always come through if I make room for Him. Obviously Satan does not want a move of the Holy Spirit, so he will attack our faith to try to discourage us from reaching out into the supernatural. This especially happens if you are ministering in a meeting where unbelief prevails. Do not allow this doubting spirit to intimidate you, but exercise your faith and push through the barriers of doubt and unbelief.

When having a service, I explain to the congregation that "by the mouth of two or three witnesses every word shall be established" (2 Cor. 13:1). If I have preached the truth, that constitutes one witness, the witness of the Word. If I ask the Holy Spirit — who is the Spirit of truth — to bear witness to the truth I have preached (see 1 John 5:6), then that constitutes the second witness. Lastly, if the Holy Spirit bears witness with our spirits (see

Rom. 8:16), then that constitutes the third witness.

I go on to explain that all doctrine is to be experienced and not merely espoused. The early church first experienced truth and then put it down into theological terms (see the Gospels, Acts and the epistles, in that order). The Holy Spirit makes God's Word real to us. The Holy Spirit's presence creates an experience in our spirits that brings deliverance to our whole being. As we ask the Holy Spirit to come, we must wait patiently for Him to appear. He is like a dove. As we stand quietly in His presence, He will descend on us. We need to rid ourselves of all distractions, skepticism and disunity. I then tell them that the Holy Spirit will come as I pray and invite Him to appear. If we create that atmosphere, we will not be disappointed.

We must bear in mind that the Holy Spirit is a person who has likes and dislikes. He is easily grieved. It is important to teach our children and adults to be sensitive to the Holy Spirit's presence. This is not the time to wander off to the bathroom or to start talking or to play with the baby. In my meetings I ask the children to get rid of their chewing gum as they come forward to pray in the Spirit. I tell them it is not possible to have their mouths full of worship if they are half full of gum.

I remember being at a conference and seeing a drama performed by some teenagers where some of them were depicting a crucifixion scene. As a number of them stood with their hands outstretched and their heads over to one side, portraying the pain and agony of the cross, one girl was chewing away on her gum. This ruined the whole drama for me, and in my opinion it did not bring glory to the

Lord.

This is why it is so important to explain to our youngsters about the Holy Spirit's ways and then bring them into a place of sensitivity to Him. As we teach the children and adults to be in unity (in one accord) when we gather together, then the Holy Spirit will come and manifest Himself (see Acts 2:1-4).

This is also not the time for some adult to jump up and quench the Holy Spirit, though some things happen during the moving of the Holy Spirit which may upset some people's church traditions or order of service. This is again why it is so important to explain that the Spirit is not bound by our limited traditions or religious concepts (see 1 Thess. 5:19, Eph. 4:30).

Remember, this is an exercise of faith. You do not have to be a superstar to bring people into the presence of God. The Holy Spirit will come upon everyone, including the children, and many unusual and wonderful manifestations will take place. We may have to stand in faith for some time, praying against spirits of distraction and encouraging the children and adults to fix their minds on the Lord. I tell them that once the Holy Spirit appears, I am not responsible for what He does, so they are not to be surprised if unusual manifestations take place, such as crying, laughing, falling down, shaking with emotional and physical healing, deliverance, repentance and salvation.

This kind of happening tends to disrupt the program, so one doesn't always know how to finish. Probably the best way to close the service is to announce that the meeting is officially closing so that those who have to leave may go. Personal ministry will continue until people's needs are met.

It is also wise to ask those who have to leave to do so quietly and reverently while the Holy Spirit is still moving. Little children sometimes cause noise and disturbance. If Satan can use them in this way to quench the Holy Spirit, he will. Take authority in the Spirit if and when this arises and explain to the children that they must behave. If you use your faith, and the anointing is upon you, you will be successful in bringing them into order.

I received a letter from a youth pastor some time ago. She was very excited. She said that she had read my book *Kids in Combat* and was very encouraged. She decided to believe for God to move on the youngsters during the youth meeting. They all went down into the sanctuary and prayed for the Lord to move. Some of the kids were giggling, and for a while nothing seemed to happen. She was just about to give up when she remembered reading in my book about the time I waited for twenty minutes for God to do something. She decided to wait it out, and suddenly the Holy Spirit moved upon some of the youngsters. They began to pray and prophesy over each other, and weep and praise God. She ended up having a revival among the youth in her church.

One time I was speaking at a Christian school in Vancouver, Canada. The students at the meeting were from the first to the twelfth grades. The principal had led the worship and found it hard to get any enthusiastic participation from the youngsters. There were about forty Asian students out of the 130 present. Most of the Asians weren't saved, and after I preached to the kids I made an appeal for salvation, hoping that some of the Asians would respond. None of them budged, so I then gave an invitation to any who wanted to receive a fresh anointing from God. A large number came up. I prayed for them and then sat down with the principal and waited for God to move.

After five or ten minutes a fifteen-year-old girl started to prophesy and pray against the demonic powers that were holding them bound, both in the school and in their homes. She went over to a teenage boy, laid hands on him and prayed. He came under conviction and began to weep. Suddenly the Spirit moved on dozens of youngsters, and they all began to minister to each other. They ended up in groups of circles with students from first through twelfth grade all ministering to one another in the Spirit.

One of the teenage boys went over to the Asian students, who were watching in awe, and prayed for one of the Asian teenage boys. Within a few minutes the boy was saved, delivered and baptized in the Holy Spirit. Except for about two students, everyone was affected. Many others were saved and filled with the Holy Spirit for the first time.

The teachers came in and cried as they saw what was happening. Then a group of the kids began to worship spontaneously and ended up marching all around the school, praising God and proclaiming that Jesus was Lord. The principal told me that the fifteen-year-old girl who had been used to set the whole thing off was slightly retarded and had been regarded by the others as socially unacceptable. "The foolishness of God is wiser than men" (1 Cor. 1:25).

# FIVE

# EXPLAINING
# SPIRITUAL GIFTS

E phesians 4:11-12 says that Christians are to be spiritually equipped for the work of service through the fivefold ministry gifts (apostle, prophet, evangelist, pastor and teacher). If we take these verses seriously, then our children must also be included in that equipping. The majority of Christians who attend Spirit-filled churches do not go beyond speaking in other tongues, and yet there are at least nine gifts listed which apparently are available to those who desire them (see 1 Cor. 12:7-11; 14:1,39).

Many teachers have divided the nine gifts into segments of three.

1. *Verbal gifts.* Messages in tongues, prophecy, interpretation of tongues. These enable us to *talk* like God.

2. *Inspirational gifts.* Word of knowledge, word of wisdom, discerning of spirits. These enable us to *think* like God.

3. *Power gifts.* Faith, working of miracles, gifts of healing. These enable us to *act* like God.

It is worth noting that there are also nine fruits of the Spirit listed in Galatians 5:22-23. We all receive encouragement to desire the fruits of the

Spirit in our lives, but there is little or no encouragement to press in to receive the gifts. So you can see that the children and youth for the most part have been left out altogether.

It is crucial to realize the fruits and the gifts do not belong to us or our children but to the Holy Spirit. As we walk in the Spirit and encourage our youngsters also, then the fruits and gifts will become evident in all of our lives. When we as a body neglect certain gifts, it can hinder our functioning in all areas. It's like the eagle, which has nine major feathers on each wing. If it loses one of them, it cannot balance itself and fly properly.

The eagle is a remarkable bird, capable of soaring to great heights as it catches the wind currents. This is comparable to Christians relying on the wind of the Holy Spirit to enable them to fulfill God's plan for their lives.

When an eagle becomes old, its feathers lose their oil and become dry. It can no longer fly. At this point it finds a safe place high up in the rocky cliffs and waits. During this period of waiting its body generates fresh oil, and new feathers grow. It becomes born anew. "Your youth is renewed like the eagle's" (Ps. 103:5). This is a picture of the fresh oil of the Holy Spirit that comes when we wait on the Lord.

I tell children that God has not called us to be chickens but eagles. Chickens spend their whole lives with their heads down, looking for grubs and worms to eat (cares of the world). They are completely earthbound, and their future is very dim. The best they can look forward to is Col. Sanders. On the other hand, eagles are majestic birds, powerful warriors, soaring to great heights and then swooping down upon their prey.

When the female eagle has its young, it eventually pushes them out of the nest from high up in the cliffs. The little eagles fall like stones, ignorant of their ability to fly. The mother eagle swoops down and catches the young eagles on her wings before they are dashed upon the rocks below. She does this several times and then finally swoops down no longer. At that time the baby eagles must spread their wings and fly to save themselves from certain death. We as Christians are expected to spread our spiritual wings and fly and not act like chickens with an earthbound mentality. We can explain to our youngsters that it's a little scary moving out in the Spirit, but it's also exciting. Although we may make mistakes, we will succeed.

The three verbal gifts (speaking in tongues, interpretation of tongues and prophecy) are God's way of speaking through a human mouthpiece (see 1 Pet. 4:11). These gifts are used mainly in a meeting context, but prophecy can be used in other situations. We know that in a Spirit-filled meeting an individual can bring forth a message in tongues, and another, the interpretation. There is no reason why children cannot do this either in children's meetings or even adult meetings.

I was at a church in East Lansing, Michigan, some years ago. The pastor had canceled the Sunday morning children's church and had the children in with the adults. During that Sunday morning service I saw a little girl about seven years of age come up to the platform and give a message in tongues and return to her seat. A few minutes later a little boy of about nine years came up and gave the interpretation. His message was very powerful. He said that as Joshua had brought the people into the promised land and brought down the walls of Jericho, so was the church to go forward and take the land for the Lord. He was really stirring up the people to be bold for God. I don't know about the others present, but I was very blessed to witness that. Of course, children have to start with receiving their own prayer language, for if they cannot pray in tongues to themselves, they will not be able to bring forth messages.

A number of children have said to me that they do not know how to speak in tongues. I tell them that neither do I. "There is no school where you can go to learn how to speak with other tongues," I tell them. "Only the Holy Spirit enables you to do that." We have to speak out with our mouths and voices, and the Holy Spirit will give us the words. The only thing that will stop us from speaking in tongues is either not to speak or to speak in English. That's because it's impossible to speak in tongues if you are not speaking out or if you are speaking out in English. Explain that to the children, and they will understand.

People often ask me about small children copying or mimicking their parents, such as speaking in tongues or praying. They wonder if they should discourage the child until he or she has a better understanding of what it means. Children will often play out roles when they are affected by what they see or hear. I personally would *not* discourage a child in these areas but would guide him in seeing the importance and significance of these things.

The logic for my actions comes partly from seeing the effects of evil on children. A lot of children have been involved in playing with ouija boards and Dungeons and Dragons. Although they are only supposed to be games, Christian parents warn their youngsters against the dangers of playing around with occult and demonic powers. If it is true that Satan can affect kids who play occult games, cannot the Holy Spirit affect our children if they play spiritual games?

I remember Andrew Culverwell, a Christian singer and songwriter, telling me that when he was a small boy he pretended to hold church meetings with his friend Terry Barge. Terry was to be the preacher, and he was to be the sinner. When Terry preached the gospel and made an appeal, Andrew came forward to receive Christ. Although they were only playing a game, Andrew recalls that that was the time when he gave his heart to the Lord.

Prophecy is very much like giving a message in tongues except this time it is in English. I remember the desire I had to prophesy after I was filled with the Holy Spirit. I wanted to do it, but I was scared I might mess up and make a fool of myself. Perhaps I would dry up in the middle of the prophecy, or it would be all wrong and not of God. Perhaps the church leaders would publicly rebuke me for being presumptuous. Finally I solved the problem. I went home, closed myself in my bedroom and began to pray. As I felt the Spirit coming upon me, I began to prophesy to myself — God speaking to me, through me. That way I learned confidence to reach out in public prophecy .

The inspirational gifts involve receiving revelation from the Spirit of God that would not be available to us in the natural realm. The word of knowledge is receiving information from God about a person or a situation. God is the source of all knowledge, and He sometimes reveals a little of that to our spirits. Some examples of the word of knowledge are Jesus with the woman at the well or Peter speaking to Ananias and Sapphira (John 4:16-18; Acts 5:1-11). In these cases the word of knowledge was not only received but also given. When I used to preach in secular schools in England, God would often give me words of knowledge for the would-be hecklers, which became a very effective way of stopping them in their tracks.

It may be that when we receive a word of knowledge, we will also need to receive a word of wisdom on when, or if, to give it out. When God gives us a revelation or a word of knowledge, we need to 1) discern who it is for, 2) know when it should be given and 3) understand whether it is for public hearing or if it should be given privately. The word of knowledge can also be used in preaching. Most of us who have been used in preaching or counseling have often experienced speaking out revelation truth by the Spirit. We had *not* thought it out or been taught it before. It just came forth by the Spirit.

A word of wisdom is a spark of divine wisdom that comes directly from God. God is the source of all wisdom; therefore, we can receive part of that wisdom as the need arises. There is a famous story about the Scottish Covenanteers, who lived some centuries ago in Scotland. These were a group of believers who were breaking the law of the land by holding religious meetings in their homes. If they were caught, they were thrown into prison. The story tells about a group of children who were on their way to a Sunday morning "cottage meeting"

They were stopped by red-coat soldiers and asked where they were going.

A little girl of about eleven years of age became their spokesperson. She was facing a problem. She could not lie because she was a Christian. But if she told the truth she would be arrested, and the people she was meeting with would also be arrested. She then received a word of wisdom. "Our older brother has died, and we are going to find out what has been left to us in His will," she replied.

"In that case, go to your business," the soldiers said. They never realized she was talking about Jesus and the Bible.

A word of wisdom can also be very appropriate in counseling situations. So much Christian counseling has just been common sense, but a word of wisdom from the Lord can make all the difference. We don't want to just give people our opinions but a word from God. We want to teach our children how to wait on God and be able give a "word in season" to their peers. Years ago preachers who were invited to speak at meetings or conventions often sat waiting on God, keeping their listeners waiting until they had received "the word of the Lord." There were plenty of good things that they could have said, but they desired something better for the people.

Because of the inexperience and immaturity of young children, they are not able to give good advice, but they can bring a word from God. Like the word of knowledge, the word of wisdom can be used when one is preaching. As in counseling one can operate in the word of wisdom, so in preaching God's wisdom often comes from the preacher's lips and afterward the preacher wonders how such wisdom could have been uttered by a mortal such as he.

Discerning of spirits is more than having spiritual discernment. A number of mature Christians, after years of experience, are able to discern accurately. Perhaps they can discern whether a person is a genuine seeker or if a young Christian is being honest in his relationship with God. The gift of discerning of spirits is not only able to do that but more. It enables the believer to discern between the Spirit of God, the human spirit and an evil spirit. Our human wisdom and understanding have limitations, so this is why we need that supernatural gift. Children's wisdom and understanding are even more limited than adults', so they need the gift operating in them even more than we do.

When we feel uncomfortable about a person, this is usually a warning that something is wrong, even if we can't put our finger on anything. If this person's presence continues to make us feel uncomfortable, we should reach out in faith for discernment. We will then find that the Lord will often reveal to us the kind of spirit operating in that person.

For the ministry of deliverance to be successful one must operate in the gift of discerning of spirits. Unfortunately, a number of fundamentalist Christians would call the work of the Spirit of God an evil spirit or a fleshly display. Because they do not believe or operate in the gifts of the spirit, they tend to judge everything according to "religious human reason." Even Spirit-filled Christians can show their immaturity when attempting to minister deliverance because of their inability to use the gift of discerning of spirits.

For example, the human spirit cannot be cast out, but it must come under the authority of the Holy Spirit. The human spirit can be so strong and rebellious in some people that for all intents and purposes it looks and behaves like an evil spirit. You might say, If that is the case, how on earth do you expect children to operate in this realm? I have mentioned in my other writings that children can — and often have — ministered deliverance to other children. The secret is that the maturity and wisdom does not come from us; it comes from God. A child who learns to hear God's voice and the prompting of the Holy Spirit will many times be accurate in his discernment and will often minister deliverance effectively to others.

If children are ministering deliverance, it is a good practice to have mature spiritual adults present. If you are in a meeting and an evil spirit manifests itself, you may have to deal with it immediately. However, do not plan to have a deliverance service without consent from the children's parents and the elders. It could cause a problem if you have a deliverance meeting without clearance and a child goes home telling her parents that she has just been delivered from fifteen demons in children's church. Deliverance is a controversial subject to some, especially the idea of a Christian having a demon.

The power gifts (faith, healing and working of miracles) can be used from time to time by believers, even though these gifts are usually attributed to special ministries such as that of evangelists and prophets. There can be times when great faith wells up in believers for a special miracle, and God moves through them in a mighty way. When little eight-year-old Zoe came out of a powerful children's meeting and saw a man in a wheelchair, she had faith for God to use her to deliver him from his six years of bondage. That special gift of faith and the gifts of healing operated through her. God sovereignly chose to use her for that situation because she was sensitive to His Spirit.

All believers have received a measure of faith (see Rom. 12:3), but most commentators agree that the faith mentioned in 1 Corinthians 12:9 is a special kind. It is the faith given to work or believe for special miracles and signs. Special miracles were given to the apostles (Acts 2:43; 19:11). As mentioned previously, these special miracles usually operate in the fivefold ministries (apostles, prophets, evangelists, pastors, teachers; see Eph. 4:11). Working of miracles is more than healing. Jesus calmed the sea, raised the dead and turned water into wine. Those were special miracles.

Most Christians have not seen many special miracles happen today, and some have never seen them at all. This does not mean God does not want to perform them, but the church at large seems to feel it has managed quite well without them and has often preached against — or warned people to beware of — such manifestations and claims.

I recently received documented evidence of what has come to be called the "signs in the sky" in the regions of Sarawak and Borneo, which comprise an island in the South China Sea. In one account some girl scouts were holding a baptismal service at a camp at Siar Beach, near Kuching, Sarawak. As each girl was being baptized in the ocean, her name was written in the sky. One, of course, can also read the account of the revival that occurred in nearby Indonesia in Mel Tari's book *Like a Mighty Wind*. The book is filled with stories of signs, wonders and miracles, even among children. As our lives become less worldly and more faithful, we will also see a great manifestation of miracles.

Healing can be manifested as Christians pray for God to heal the sick. At other times, however, the spirit of healing will flow through a vessel, such as a child or adult. Many people, including children, have felt God's power flow through their hands as they have prayed for others. One can pray for someone to receive the baptism of the Holy Spirit, and through combined faith God will answer and they will receive. There can be other times when a divine impartation of the Holy Spirit is given to the recipient either directly or through another believer who is a willing channel of God's power.

Healing can also be combined with other gifts, such as the word of knowledge. I remember many years ago Kathie and I were praying for a woman who was a diabetic. We sensed the Lord telling us that the reason she was not getting healed was due to bitterness and unforgiveness. We asked her if she had unforgiveness in her heart, but she denied it. We continued to press her, and she finally said that she resented her mother. When she was a baby, her mother dropped her and she went into shock, which apparently caused her diabetes. We told her she must forgive her mother to receive her healing. She finally repented with tears and asked the Lord to forgive her, and she was subsequently healed.

We know that the gifts are given by the Spirit individually as He wills (1 Cor. 12:11), but we are

47

also encouraged to desire them (1 Cor. 14:1,39). So it is important for us to cooperate in our faith with the Holy Spirit. I personally believe that the gifts of the Holy Spirit (apart from personal tongues, which one can operate at any time) are available for any believer to use as the need arises. This means that we do not possess all the gifts, but during our lifetime we can operate in all of them.

To clarify, we may all prophesy (1 Cor. 14:24,31), but we are not all called to be prophets (1 Cor. 12:29). We can all witness (Luke 12:8), but we are not all called to be evangelists (Eph. 4:11). We can all pray for the sick (Mark 16:17-18), but we don't all have a healing ministry (1 Cor. 12:30). I believe Paul makes it plain when he says, "Are all apostles? Are all prophets? Are all teachers? Are all workers of miracles? Do all have gifts of healing? Do all speak with tongues? Do all interpret?" (1 Cor. 12:29-30). He then goes on to say, "I wish you all spoke with tongues, but even more that you prophesied" (1 Cor. 14:5).

At first these verses seem contradictory, but we must remember two things. We have to differentiate between the office of a prophet (Eph. 4:11) and believers prophesying for edification, exhortation and comfort (1 Cor. 14:3,5,31). We also need to distinguish between tongues for personal edification (1 Cor. 14:4; Jude 20) and giving a message in tongues with interpretation for the edification of the church (1 Cor. 14:27).

God is able to use anyone in the gifts if they are open, but not everyone who attends a meeting needs to feel compelled to minister through the gifts every time they attend. In fact, Paul indicates that in a meeting context we need to confine the exercising of gifts to a limited number so that things will not get out of hand (see 1 Cor. 14:26-30,40).

Some time ago I ministered in a church in Ohio, and a number of the youngsters asked their teachers if I could instruct them about the gifts of the Holy Spirit. There was real desire and enthusiasm among these kids, not only to learn more about this subject but to participate in exercising spiritual gifts. I see no reason why our children and teens cannot be recruited for a "school of the Holy Spirit" in our local churches. Obviously those who lead the sessions would need to have firsthand experience. This is why it is important that our workers are anointed and spiritually equipped, and are not just volunteers reading lessons out of Sunday school material.

As I mentioned in the first chapter, people are tripartite beings. I say the same thing to the children. When I minister to them, I tell them they are made up of three parts: body, mind and spirit. They eat and exercise to develop their bodies, and they go to school to develop their minds. They would be very concerned if in two or three year's time they were still the same size physically and their intellect had not developed. They would think something was seriously wrong with them. Yet so many are content to have a pygmy or stunted spirit.

# SIX

# HEARING GOD'S VOICE

The church is ordained of God to help children develop their spirits. This is more than a Christian education program. This involves increasing their spiritual potential by teaching them how to know the Word of God and believe it. We must encourage them to hear God's voice for themselves by developing a spiritual relationship with Him. It also means putting them into the school of the Holy Spirit, where they can be trained in spiritual gifts, intercession, worship, power-evangelism and obedience to God's ways.

Much of this must come by revelation to their spirits. We don't merely want to educate their minds but to impart to their spirits. The apostle Paul, writing to the Ephesians, said:

> [I] do not cease to...[make] mention of you in my prayers: that the God of our Lord Jesus Christ, the Father of glory, may give to you the spirit of wisdom and revelation in the knowledge of Him, the eyes of your understanding being enlightened; that you may know what is the hope of His calling, what are the riches of the glory of His

inheritance in the saints (Eph. 1:16-18).

Let us remember that these passages refer to our children as much as they do to us. This is more than giving our youngsters information. Too many children know the right answers but have a very limited relationship with the supernatural God.

We can see that our concept of Christian education must be more than merely giving our students information. We cannot use exactly the same principles as secular education. The dynamics of Christianity revolve around an experience with Jesus Christ and the power of the Holy Spirit. We as adults must be able to impart — as well as teach on — spiritual gifts and so on. If we are limited in our supernatural walk with God, then we will not be able to bring our children into any more than we have experienced. Learning to follow the Holy Spirit is more important than following the curriculum. This does not mean we should *not* seek out or design first-class teaching materials for children, but, remember, church is more than Sunday school. We could be in danger of having only teachers and programs available for our kids, rather than anointed vessels.

As previously mentioned, to equip the saints effectively they must be exposed to all of the five ministry gifts (Eph. 4:11-12). There is a story about a man who read a sermon by John Wesley. When Wesley preached it in his day, marvelous results happened and many souls were converted. The man decided that if he learned the sermon by heart and preached it, he would experience the same results as Wesley. Needless to say, when he preached the same message, nothing happened. That's because the anointing was not in the sermon but in God's vessel, John Wesley.

I believe the Lord desires to communicate to us more than we expect. Many of us are still waiting for a flash of lightning and a clap of thunder, followed by a booming voice from the clouds, before we will be convinced that God is speaking. Although that is possible, God usually speaks quietly to our spirits in such a way that many times we think it is just our own thoughts. If our children exercise their faith and respond to those gentle promptings of the Holy Spirit and develop a sensitivity to God's voice, they will be amazed at how exciting their Christian lives will become.

At my meetings I have noticed that many children and teens have a real experience with the Holy Spirit for the first time in their lives. I believe the reason for this is that I teach them to stand still and wait for the Holy Spirit to communicate with them. Most of our children are so busy running that they have not learned how to wait on God. Even if we have them praying, we don't give them time to listen for God's answer. They need to see that silence is not a bad thing, and noise is not always necessary.

We as adults have the same problem. Many times we have great prayer meetings where we do much talking and little listening. Even when we do attempt to listen we are often not exercising our faith to believe for God to speak to us. As we get involved with the school of the Spirit with the children, we will all learn together, even by our mistakes. It will become a very exciting adventure as we develop our spiritual ears.

If you are leading a youth or children's meeting,

one spiritual exercise you can do is to have the youngsters face each other in pairs. Tell them to pray in the Spirit, asking God to give them a word of encouragement or exhortation for their partner. Explain that God will often speak to them through various ways; for example, dreams, words and so on. If some do not get anything, don't let them be discouraged. A number will receive something for their partners. After they have ministered to each other, ask them if they believe that God spoke to them through their partner. You will be surprised with the results. This is only the first phase of the exercise. Explain to them that this can be developed into a life-style. As they grow in this, they will not only minister to other Christian children, but they will at certain times have something for adults and even unbelievers.

Some adults might protest this simple act of faith by saying, "You are just teaching our children to believe that whatever comes into their heads must be of God". We are not so naive as to accept everything given as from God. Remember, this is a *school* of the Spirit! We are learning, so there will be mistakes. Not all dreams, visions, prophecies, promptings and leadings are from the Holy Spirit. On the other hand, some folks are so afraid of being led astray that they will not be led at all. They seem to have more confidence that the devil will speak to them or that their own imaginations will deceive them than faith that God's ability will keep them out of error (see Luke 11:10-13). Some leaders so emphasize the "decently and in order" that they will not allow "all things to be done" (1 Cor. 14:40).

# SEVEN

# EXERCISING SPIRITUAL GIFTS

What the youngsters give out will have to be judged (1 Cor. 14:29), but not without love and encouragement. As infants first learn to walk in the natural, they fall a few times, but they eventually make it. When infants first fall down, they don't decide they were not made for walking and go back to crawling. God did not create us like cats or dogs to go around on all fours, but He created us to walk upright on two legs. In the spiritual realm it is the same. When we are born again and filled with the Holy Spirit, we are created by God to have a spiritual walk, even if we fall a few times.

I remember an evangelist friend of mine who, when he first started to move out in the Holy Spirit, prayed for the sick. He recounts that the first three people he prayed for died. He said, "I thought I had a ministry of death." But he did not quit. He continued on, and God gave him a wonderful healing ministry. As most kids have been taught, if at first you don't succeed, try, try again.

We are teaching our children to live and walk in the Spirit (Gal. 5:25). If they receive the revelation of this wonderful experience, their relationship with each other will improve dramatically. They will no longer judge each other after the flesh (Rom 8:1; 2 Cor. 5:16; Gal. 5:25-26). As our children grow in their relationship with the Holy Spirit, they will learn to use spiritual gifts in places other than church meetings. They will become more aware that God speaks to them at many different times and in various situations.

In the book of Hebrews we read, "For we have not a high priest which cannot be touched with the feeling of our infirmities; but was in all points tempted like as we are, yet without sin" (Heb. 4:15, KJV). From this scripture we must deduce that our Lord, as our high priest, is involved with our weaknesses and infirmities. He is not merely sympathizing but identifying Himself with us and feeling our pain. I know there are times when Christ feels the pain of a person. Because Christ dwells in us (Rom. 8:9-11; Col. 1:27) and we are members of His body (1 Cor. 12:27), we are also able to feel that pain. This is another way in which the word of knowledge can operate through us — by touching certain parts of our bodies and indicating the physical need in the person being prayed for. Many well-known preachers with healing ministries have functioned in this way. Through this type of word of knowledge children are able to minister or pray for people in need — with exciting results.

A few years ago when my eldest daughter, Faith, was about nine, she began having chest pains. Kathie asked her if this was a physical problem or if God was giving her a word of knowledge by touching her body. As Faith prayed about this, she kept getting a burden for a friend of ours named Ron. Kathie and Faith began to pray for Ron, not knowing anything about his situation. In a while the burden lifted.

A few days later Faith started having pains in her chest again, coupled with a burden for Ron. Faith and Kathie went into intercession again for Ron until the burden lifted. They finally decided to call Ron to find out what was going on. He told them he had had a heart attack a few months ago, and the doctor had warned him about stress. He had been going through a very stressful situation recently because of three houses he had built but had been unable to sell. The bank was putting pressure on him regarding his loans. Because of all this he had been getting chest pains again and was fearful of having another heart attack.

Suddenly the Lord delivered him from fear and stress and gave him faith to believe for the sale of his properties. Within a short time he sold the houses and was able to satisfy the loans. The Christ in a little girl was able to minister to Ron because she was open to God's Spirit.

Recently Kathie had a burden to pray for a well-known prophet. As she began to pray for him, she asked Lisa, our ten-year-old, to pray with her. After a while Kathie asked Lisa if she had received anything from the Lord. Lisa said she had a vision of a deflated football being snatched by different teams. She went on to say the Lord showed her that the football represented the prophet and the different teams were people coming against him. The reason the ball was deflated was because he was feeling sorry for himself. Kathie wrote him a letter explaining the vision.

A few days later he called to say he had received the letter and that what Lisa had seen was correct.

He had spent two days repenting for feeling sorry for himself. He said, "Your little daughter is a seer."

A simple act of faith by a little girl spoke to a prophet. As you encourage children to move out in the word of knowledge, they may go up to someone in a service and just say a simple, "God says He loves you". You may think that's not very profound, but never underestimate the way God works. That person may have been so harassed by the devil that they felt totally abandoned by God, and that simple word brought their deliverance.

It is amazing how God used young Samuel to minister to Eli the priest. Samuel was dedicated to the Lord by Hannah, his mother, and served Eli from his childhood through adolescence (1 Sam. 1:28; 2:11). You will also remember that Eli's sons were corrupt (1 Sam. 2:12). In 1 Samuel 3:1-18 we read how God began to speak to young Samuel, but at first he thought it was Eli calling him. Eli realized that God was calling Samuel and told him how to answer God. Eli then told Samuel to let him know what God was saying, but when Samuel received the message, he was afraid to tell Eli. Remember, Samuel was just a young lad, and Eli was his mentor. Eli insisted on knowing, so Samuel obeyed and confirmed the word of rebuke and judgment from the Lord. God not only spoke through a youngster but used him in this case to rebuke an elder.

# EIGHT

# GOD'S WAY OF COMMUNICATING

How many ways does God communicate to us today? I know of four major ways.

1. He speaks through His revealed written Word found in Scripture.

2. He speaks to our spirits (as previously mentioned). Let us remember to explain to our children that God never contradicts His written Word when He speaks to our spirits.

3. He speaks through other people. This is usually through mature Christians such as pastors, preachers and spiritual brothers and sisters. It is also possible for God to speak to us through a non-believer, because He is not limited in whom He can use. Remember the donkey and the false prophet (2 Pet. 2:16, Num. 22:28, 23:19, 24:1).

4. God can speak to us through our circumstances. If we are not believing His Word and are not listening to our spirits and are not open to hear from our spiritual peers, then God will often get our attention through adverse circumstances. Absalom called Joab to come to him, but he could not get Joab to answer, so he set his barley fields on fire. That got Joab's attention (2 Sam. 14:29-32). Let us encourage our children to learn to obey

God's voice rather than cause themselves trouble because of stubbornness and rebellion.

God has made plenty of provision in His word for us and our children to communicate with Him. We are told that we have been given the mind of Christ (see 1 Cor. 2:16). We need to grow in our experience of having a new mind, so we are told to *let* the same mind be in us which was also in Christ Jesus (see Phil. 2:5). We are again commanded to be *renewed* in the Spirit of our mind (see Eph. 4:23), so this is obviously an experiential process. As someone once said, "Learn to speak and think the way of the kingdom."

If your child were to emigrate to another country, he would eventually pick up the accent and habits of the people there. Upon arriving he would still sound like an American and desire American-style food. Eventually his accent would change, and he would adapt to the food of the country and even learn to like it. The same principles apply to the spiritual realm. As one grows in the kingdom of God and learns to walk strong in the Spirit, the old worldly ways and desires decrease until sinful worldly attractions have lost their power over the believer.

When I explain to youngsters how to recognize God's voice, I use an analogy of receiving a phone call from an old friend. Young Jimmy who moved out of town three years ago has suddenly returned. He calls up his old playmate Billie, but he doesn't tell him who's calling. Billie fails to recognize Jimmy's voice because they have not communicated for three years. He finally tells Billie who he is, they chat and then Jimmy hangs up. A few days later Jimmy calls again, and after a few seconds

Billie recognizes his voice. Then Jimmy begins to call Billie on a regular basis, and as soon as Jimmy says, "Hi, Billie, how are you doing?" Billie recognizes him. Communication brings familiarity.

In the past we have taught our children to know about God, but now they are going to *know Him*. "This is life eternal, that they might know thee the only true God, and Jesus Christ, whom thou hast sent" (John 17:3, KJV). I like the way Dian Layton paraphrases Daniel 11:32 for kids in her book *Soldiers With Little Feet*. "They that know their God shall have mega-muscles and go on adventures."

The Christian life is an adventure. Serving God is more than keeping rules and being good. With all the mistakes, mess-ups, hassles, disappointments and failures, it is still worthwhile. Our children can be taught to know God and have a powerful relationship with Him. They can become bold in their faith and stay excited about spiritual things. Smith Wigglesworth once said that he got more excitement in two hours of serving the Lord than the average Christian does in six months. Let's tell our youngsters God has not called them to be average Christians but mighty ones.

To summarize, I believe there are three fundamental steps to our children's spiritual growth:

1. They experience a real baptism of the Holy Spirit.

2. They are taught how to function in the gifts of the Spirit.

3. They cultivate a close spiritual walk with God.

Is this possible for young children and teens? Yes! It's difficult; it's challenging; but it's possible.

Teachers, here are some steps to follow.

1. Covet God's anointing! "And the yoke will be destroyed because of the anointing" (Is. 10:27).

2. Learn about spiritual gifts. "Now concerning spiritual gifts, brethren, I do not want you to be ignorant" (1 Cor. 12:1).

3. Exercise your faith with the youngsters and realize that the Holy Spirit in them desires to function in their lives and experience. Pray with them for a mighty baptism.

4. Organize a school of the Spirit and enroll those who want to grow spiritually.

Persevere until you have broken through with the children and a spirit of revival is operating. Then continue to persevere for a great harvest of souls.

## MATERIALS AVAILABLE FROM
## GOOD NEWS FELLOWSHIP MINISTRIES
### By David Walters

***Kids in Combat*** - David shows how to train children and teens in spiritual power and bring them into the anointing for ministry.(Parents, teachers and children/youth pastors).

***Children Aflame*** - Amazing accounts of children from the journals of the great Methodist preacher John Wesley in the 1700's and David's own accounts with children and youth.

***Anointing and You*** - What we must do to receive, sustain, impart, and channel the Revival Anointing for renewal/revival, and to pass it on to the younger generation.

***Worship fur Dummies*** - David Walters calls himself a dummy in the area of praise and worship, but he knows the ways of the Holy Spirit.

***Radical Living in a Godless Society*** - Our ungodly Society really targets our children and youth. How do we cope with this situation?

### CHILDREN'S BIBLE STUDY BOOKS

***Armor of God*** - Children's illustrated Bible study on Ephesians 6:14-18 (ages 6-14 years).

***Fruit of the Spirit***- Children's illustrated Bible study on Gal 5:19-23 (ages 7-15 years).

***Fact or Fantasy***- Children's illustrated Bible study on Christian apologetics. How to defend your faith (ages 8-15 years).

***Being a Christian***- Children's illustrated Bible study on what it really means to be a Christian (ages 6-15 years).

***Children's Prayer Manual***- Children's Illustrated study on prayer (ages 8-15 years).

***Available in Fall, 2005:***
***Gifts of the Spirit***- Children's Illustrated Bible study on the Gifts (ages 7-15 years).

**TAPES & VIDEOS AVAILABLE**

## By Kathie Walters

*Celtic Flames* -Read the exciting accounts of other famous Fourth & Fifth Century Celtic Christians: Patrick, Brendan, Cuthbert, Brigid and others.

*Columba - The Celtic Dove* - Read about the prophetic and miraculous ministry of this famous Celtic Christian, filled with supernatural visitations.

*Living in the Supernatural* - Kathie believes that the supernatural realm, the angels, miracles, and signs and wonders are the spiritual inheritance of every believer, as in the early church. She tells how to embrace and enter our inheritance.

*Parenting by the Spirit* - The author shows how she raised her children by listening to the Holy Spirit rather than her emotions.

*The Spirit of False Judgment* - Dealing with Heresy Hunters. Sometimes things are different from what we perceive them to be.

*The Visitation* - An account of two visitations from the Lord that Kathie experienced. One lasted for seven days and the other for 3 ½ weeks. An account also of a visitation her daughter, Faith had when she was just 17 years old.

*Angels Watching Over You* - Did you know that the angels of God are sent to minister to you and with you. They are meant to be a normal part of the life of every Christian

*The Bright and Shining Revival* - The praying men and women of the Hebrides clung to the promise that if they sought Him, He would HEAL THEIR LAND and the power of God descended on the communities of these Scottish Islands.

*Seer List* What is a Seer Anointing? How is it manifested?

*Elitism and the False Shepherding Spirit* - Elitism And It's Devastating Results(Control, Manipulation, False Shepherding Spirit, Spirit of Abortion and Grief)

*Health Related Mindsets* What are Health related Mindsets? Recommended for Mature Christians not for the new convert!

For further information or order forms
please call or write:
### Good News Fellowship Ministries
*220 Sleepy Creek Rd.
Macon Georgia 31210
Phone (478)757-8071 fax (478) 757-0136
e-mail: goodnews@reynoldscable.net
http://www.goodnews.netministries.org*

# RAISING A GENERATION OF ANOINTED CHILDREN AND YOUTH

## TRAINING AND EQUIPPING SEMINAR

*Equipping Parents, Youth Pastors, Sunday School Teachers and Children's Workers*

The churches in your area can experience one of these dynamic seminars. Author and speaker David Walters imparts a fresh vision and anointing to parents and to those who work with children and youth. Walters says:

*Children are baptized in the Holy Spirit to do much more than play, be entertained or listen to a few moral object lessons.*

*The average church-wise child can be turned around and set on fire for God.*

*Christian teenagers do not have to surrender to peer pressure; they can become the peers.*